MAKING A FAST BUCK
AND OTHER ENGLISH EXPRESSIONS

by Andrew Niccol *pictures* by Stephen Woodman

SPHERE BOOKS LIMITED

First published in Great Britain by Sphere Books Ltd 1986
27 Wright's Lane, London W8 5TZ

Printed and bound in Finland by WSOY

Changing a light bulb.

Making small talk.

A soap opera.

Seeing how the other half lives.

Having a drink in the Queen's Arms.

Terminal cancer.

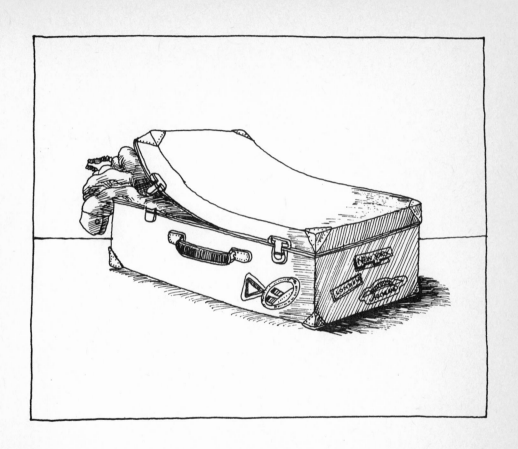

An open and shut case.

Feeling a new man.

Keeping your food down.

An ego trip.

A bit of all right.

Bringing someone to their senses.

Food that doesn't agree with you.

Getting to the bottom of something.

A rock video.

A salad bar.

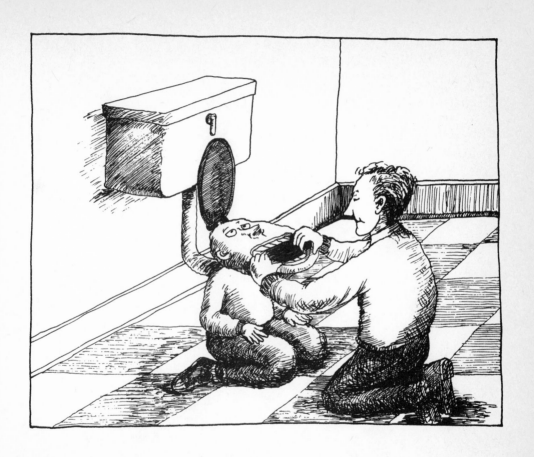

Making a convenience of someone.

Getting high on drugs.

Going through an awkward stage.

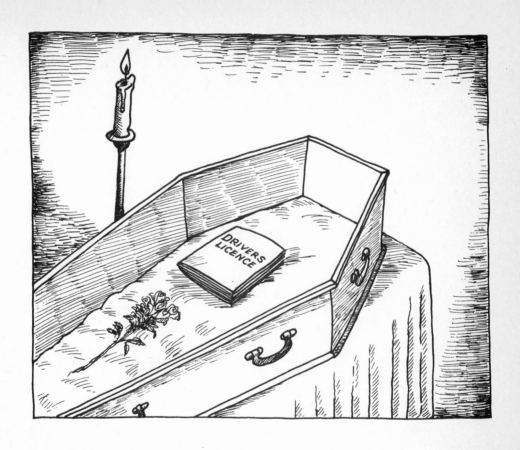

An expired licence.

The power behind the throne.

A bachelor pad.

Knowing a place like the back of your hand.

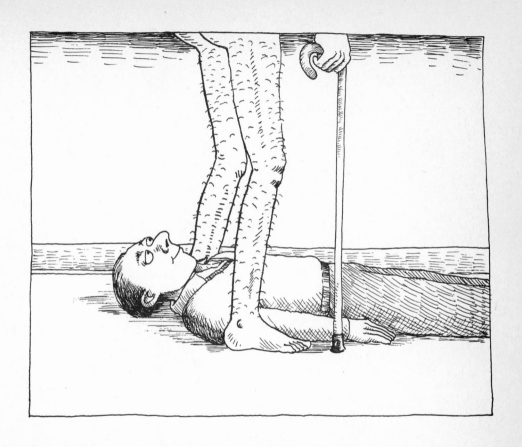

Looking up an old friend.

A peer group.

Quitting while you're ahead.

The menstrual cycle.

Using strong language.

Watching a load of rubbish on TV.

Scratching your bum.

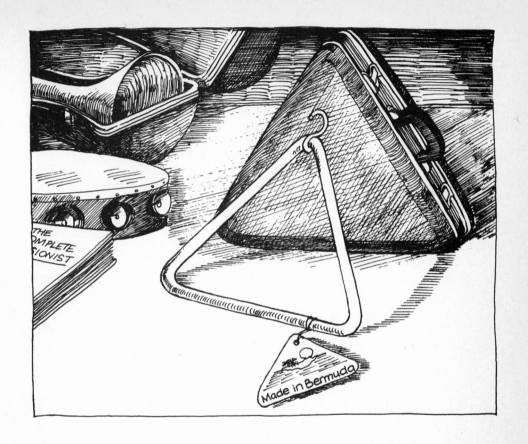

The Bermuda triangle.

Getting over an illness.

Having a drink on the house.

Making a fast buck.

A concrete suggestion.

Poetry in motion.

Having dishpan hands.

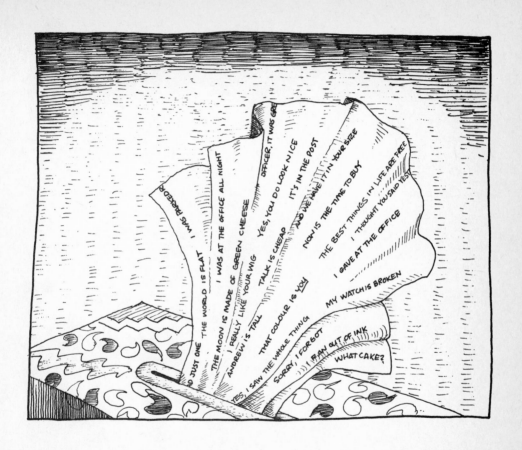

A tissue of lies.

A marriage of convenience.

Driving a point home.

An animal lover.

Putting your back out.

A communist plot.

Cultured pearls.

A show of hands.

Drawing a blank.